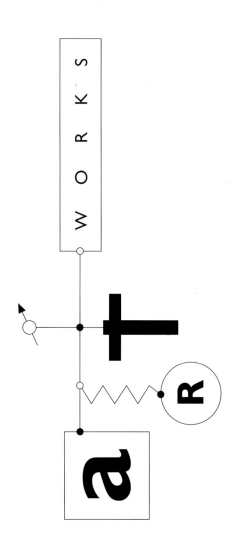

The Education Project
New York City

*This book would not have been possible
without the generous support of:*

**Lannan Foundation
Polaroid Corporation**

Additional funding provided by:

Paula Cooper Gallery
Pace/McGill Gallery

Editor: Carole Kismaric

Designer: Mark Randall

Black-and-white photography: Shelley Wood

Printing supervision: Red Ink Productions

Printed in Iceland

© 1993 Art Works/The Education Project

Library of Congress Catalog Card Number: 93-72047

ISBN: 0-9637322-0X

*Art Works Exhibition
The International Center of Photography
New York City
July – September 1993*

Contents

Too Long Apart

The Polaroid photograph is the teenager of photography. Young, popular, quick and slick, the Polaroid technique thrives on anticipation, risk and surprise. Like kids, Polaroid photographs are unrefined yet immediate. This is a photography bold and fragile. So it fits, The Education Project pairing ten professional New York artists with ten inner-city teenagers to make pictures at the Polaroid 20 x 24 Studio in Soho.

Genuine collaboration is a coming together of people to make something that would have been impossible to create alone. Elementary art partnerships join the work of two or more people together to form a single creation. A more elaborate structure for collaboration can be seen in the performing arts, where a group of individuals performs a work created by a dominant author or maestro. But isn't more than a combined effort required? A dialogue, a communication, a connection that transforms the participants can occur. Deep collaboration compels us to see ourselves through others. Truly collaborative works of art are commitments in time and space, cause and effect at once, even a form of love.

The exhibition *Art Works* suggests a new approach to team effort. But collaborations of any kind can be arduous, particularly when older well known artists work with nervous, unknown novices, who are still searching for their own voices. Anyone expecting pure equality in talent, skill and give will be disappointed; artistic cooperation is never that simple.

The Polaroid photographs born of the unlikely duos in *Art Works* look like genuine exchanges, because they are so unpredictable. Rich with give and take, none of the prints wear the signature styles of the artists. None looks like an "at-risk" teenager. All of the photographs do possess an odd sense of theater a tableaux with the clumsy discomfort that accompanies any intimate sharing of thoughts and feelings between strangers from another age, another kind of life.

Self-representation, like art, isn't easy, especially for teenagers who are developing an identity independent of their parents and institutions. Not only do young people deal with the restraints of race and class, they must withstand the disdain society holds against most people their age. The stereotyping of "at-risk" youth is total; many kids become what the mass media says they are.

Keenly divided by sex, the roles to be played are familiar: young men are gang-star rappers, bare-chested warriors, sports super heroes or James Dean clones. Young woman appear again and again as impossibly glamorous fashion models fractured through prisms; aqueous, feline nymphs floating over a misty land of sequins, pink and mauve.

In the popular imagination, the creative artist is also a type – an isolated, driven, wild, selfish, male, white individual who owes no responsibility to anyone or anything outside of the needy world of his own craft. Against these delusions, art can be a most powerful instrument for renewing the identity, pride and vision that are required to become a whole person.

So what's to be done? To simply hand students the tools of art, then issue the great liberal command, "Express yourself!" is fatuous, cruel and dismissive. Most young people, particularly teenagers from the poor public schools in the inner city, have not been taught the vocabulary of forms, techniques and concepts necessary to make works of art that escape the quicksand of cliché. Denied materials, training and opportunities for making genuine poetry, many teenagers wishing to be artists are strangers to revelation. Instead they embrace the thin, flat caricatures of original human beings. To allow our young people to turn themselves into cartoons is pernicious and wrong. To challenge the stereotypes on both sides takes time, courage, a love of change, a love of art.

Art Works is a cause for encouragement and celebration. Here, before our eyes, mature professionals and wide-eye beginners take a crucial giant step together outside their traditional social roles. Protected by the armor of new jack gear and macho poses, John Divola and Ishah B. Miah invent a new media type that is alarming in its blurring of reality and fiction. Arieana works with Felix Gonzalez-Torres making photographs of her diaries – writing so achingly personal, so private, it becomes universal; it becomes art.

Chuck Close combines his life-long interest in representing the human face with Lee Hines' wish to unite how he looks with how he feels. The alchemy of photography gives both the possibility, adventure and hope of transformation. Kenlly Rodriguez and Laurie Simmons together create photographs of, well, a giving tree? Photos of desirable objects – sneakers, designer outfits, a perfume bottle in the shape of a heart – dangle from branches. Grown in a consumer culture where you are what you own, this tree is not just a portrait of the artist as a young woman, but a catalog of our times as well.

Almost all teenagers in America practice the medium of collage on their bedroom walls. In Richard M. and John Reuter's work, fragments of photographs of Carl Lewis, Magic Johnson and others integrate in a pantheon of personal heroes. In her portrait by Timothy Greenfield-Sanders, Helena refuses to be scrutinized. Instead, she checks us out, reads us, looks out from behind the glossy surface of the Polaroid print with a fierce determination. In contrast, Helena's portrait of Greenfield-Sanders fixes the artist in a moment of intense self-examination.

There is an important coming together in three photographs taken with Paul McGinnis by Andres Serrano. With a brother on one side, and a mother on the other, Paul becomes central to the family's gaze. There is a sense that these photographs portray not only three faces, but a showdown.

Carla Weber and Zahrah L. make photographs that are like the looking glass Alice had to pass through on her way to Wonderland. These complex pictures reflect dreams and wishes through a jumble of colors and references. Fernando Ruiz's knowledge of graffiti technique is combined with William Wegman's familiarity with the Polaroid medium to create a raucous, split-second homage to fun and world peace. Jean Vong and Jennifer R. are the architects of a new teenage Atlantis – a secret, comforting, underwater world built out of many little objects – fortune cookies, plastic dolphins, smiley faces – things from childhood that may all too soon have to be left behind.

So what's happening here? The benefits to the young people are obvious. These ten kids have had the chance to recognize, challenge and transform their imaginations. They've been exposed to a quality work situation, where what they do and how they conduct themselves matters. They've seen how things get done. How art gets made. The impact of these brief encounters cannot be underestimated.

While the lives of the students have changed, the professionals are the ones most enriched by this experience. For these ten artists to work with kids from neighborhoods, worlds away from Soho, even if only for a day, connects minds and hearts too long apart. As artists begin to engage with people as participants in the creative process, and as kids learn that making is more gratifying than consuming, differences in history, culture, education and taste can be acknowledged, then transcended.

What is most exciting about *Art Works*? This project is important because collaboration of this sort – this new way of making art – has finally, powerfully begun. Usually separated by disparate social, cultural and economic backgrounds, young people and fine artists have come together not as students and teachers, not as assistants and auteurs – but as partners. This project should not stand alone. In taking these pictures, artists and teens have crossed boundaries more presumed than real. The photographs of *Art Works* bring us all together on the common ground of art.

Tim Rollins

Chuck Close + Lee Hines

When I first started working with Sheila we did a project with video. It was very interesting to me, because I always wanted to do something with a camera. I felt that this was a start for me to show people how I feel inside. I felt that it was time to show people that I was ready to take on the world and show them that I could do it.

Sheila made me feel like I was one of them, and she gave me a chance, and I quote, "I won't let her down." Just before this project came up I had just finish doing a part in the *Malcolm X* movie, and it was a good feeling to know where I was coming from. So when the time came for this project, I was ready. The name of my project is "Four Horsemen," which consists of the heart, strength, mind and courage. I did the project with the help of a very good friend, Mr. Close, a very wise man. He has a style that makes him so amazing, and it caught my eyes and made me want to work harder to become where he is at.

When I touched the camera I felt like it was a part of me that I'd never felt before. It was like magic. After that I was very happy to work with the camera. I hope that this work can lead on to something better. I am about to do a project with waterfalls and mountain pictures and a lot more things to come.

Lee Hines

This collaboration was more self-effacing than most of the other collaborations I've been involved in, where both sides have some sense of legitimacy that comes from feeling a part of something. Both the difficulty and pleasure of working with Lee were rooted in the same issue – how to facilitate his ideas and vision without overwhelming him or pushing how I thought the work should look.

Becoming an artist is a long and lonely evolution. Those moments, when someone makes a favorable comment or takes you seriously, keep you going, sustain you. It is impossible to predict whether Lee or any young person will become an artist. He certainly has the intelligence and talent, but I do have the feeling it was a special event for him. You want these projects to work every time. If in one case someone's life has been changed a little, it's successful.

Chuck Close

Chuck Close + **Lee Hines** *Diptych*

John Divola + Ishah B. Miah

I had a very memorable experience with The Education Project. The project gave me a great opportunity to learn about the art of photography. Now I think I'd have a much better idea of how to make an album cover, if I ever make it to vinyl. I've been working on music for three-and-a-half years. I am a local hip-hop artist from the Lower East Side of Manhattan. My group's name is the Body Snatchers. My stage name is War Tech, and my D.J.'s name is Sam Goody. My brother Salim use to be my Rap partner, but ever since he passed away I've been solo. I've tried to join with several other artists from around the way, but I didn't feel comfortable so I departed from them. Here I am back to square one. Before I end this essay, I'd like to thank my homeboy Lee, John Divola and Sheila for giving me the chance of a lifetime to be a part of an art exhibit. If I never make it in the record business, I still have this memorable experience to cherish as my life continues.

Ishah B. Miah

It would be arrogant and false for me to claim that in the few days I spent with Ishah I became any sort of mentor or that I was any significant influence. I was delighted at the way our work turned out, and I found this to be a nourishing and engaging encounter. It is important to give a voice and an opportunity to individuals who have been frozen out, and this project is a symbolic step in that direction. The project was also a wonderful opportunity to bring artists together with individuals that they might not ordinarily meet. I believe what really effects these young people are the ongoing relationships that other people have with them, who support and believe in their promise every day. I hope that this project can make some small contribution to those efforts.

John Divola

John Divola + **Ishah B. Miah**

John Reuter + Richard M.

We started with some small collages Richard had made of sports figures and a self-portrait collage. The Polaroid 20 x 24 camera and its large-scale prints became the metaphor for the larger-than-life qualities of Richard's sports heroes. By also rendering his self-portrait on a big scale, I wanted to make him equal with his heroes, to help him think of himself as a hero. Perhaps the chance to work on this special camera, and the acknowledgement of his talent and worth, went some way toward boosting Richard's self-image, toward enlarging it.

John Reuter

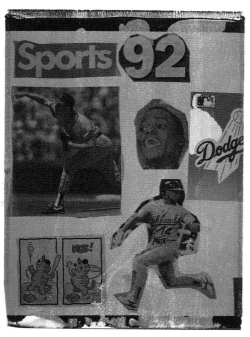

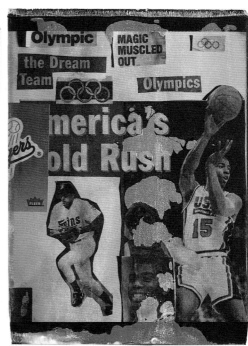

John Reuter + **Richard M.** *left: Diptych, right: Self-Portrait*

Timothy Greenfield-Sanders + Helena C.

The amazing thing about the Polaroid camera is the immediacy of the process to see someone's portrait seconds after you've taken the picture. I was moved by Helena's shock of awareness at seeing the image develop before her eyes, because it was so similar to my first experience in a dark-room. And, it's wonderful to bring people into a world they don't know.

Timothy Greenfield-Sanders

I always wanted to photograph my brother Javier, because he's always been there for me. When times have been bad he's been my silent support.

Helena C.

I'm really proud of my sister's accomplishments – she's great. I know she can make it.

Javier

Timothy Greenfield-Sanders + **Helena C.** *Diptych*

Andres Serrano + Paul McGinnis

The first time I met Paul I didn't realize he was only thirteen years old. He was with his mother Joanna, a loving mother who wants the best for her children. And Paul, being a young man, is beginning to have his own ideas about what is best for him. The next time we met, Paul brought his older brother, Brian. We had lunch, and it occurred to me that the two brothers were either fighting or horsing around. "We joke," Paul explained, "but we don't communicate." I suggested Paul do a family portrait, confronting family issues. He agreed but questioned why his mother could not be the central panel. "This time," I said, "You have to be the center of attention." I hope Paul McGinnes grows up to be a fine young artist, and if he doesn't, I hope he'll remember the day we spent at the Polaroid studio.

Andres Serrano

I want to say thank you to Andres and Janeil for making this experience possible for me. It was real special and something I will never forget. My photograph from *The New York Times* is hanging on my bedroom wall.

I feel proud that I was involved in this project, and it made me feel happy. I didn't think that I could do it until it was done. The project means alot and makes me feel good.

Paul McGinnis

The Education Project

Andres Serrano + **Paul McGinnis** *Triptych*

He agreed but questioned why his mother could
not be the central panel. 'This time,'
I said, "You have to be the center of attention."

Andres Serrano

Laurie Simmons + Kenlly Rodriguez

I quickly realized that the success of this collaboration depended upon my hanging back and not hovering over Kenlly. This was not a student-teacher relationship, and it didn't take much to get her to act on her many ideas. My presence gave her confidence.

Working with Kenlly stirred up some of my vivid memories of being a teenager. I recalled how movies and fashion magazines held all the promises of the future. We found that we were speaking a similar language through pictures.

Laurie Simmons

It was wonderful working with The Education Project. I honestly loved it. Laurie Simmons was a pleasure to work with; she gave her opinions, and I gave mine. To me my picture is about the beauty of nature, the tree. The clothing represents the great fashion in our world. The Polaroid 20 x 24 camera made the pictures seem real. There are many other talented kids out there who also wish to participate in something like this. That is why I think there should be more programs like this one.

Kenlly Rodriguez

Felix Gonzalez -Torres + Arieana R.

This project was a very interesting thing for me. I like taking pictures and being creative; it gave me a way of expressing my feelings. From the beginning, Felix made me feel I was the best. Like I had nothing to worry about. I met a lot of nice people who made me feel like the boss of this project. Felix has encouraged me to go ahead and make one of my goals to make a good future for myself.

I want to dedicate this project to Toniann, my buddy. She told me I was special and encouraged me to do this project. I thought she said it just to make me feel good. Now I know she said it because it's true. The reason I say this is because everyone made me feel so special. So now I believe it.

Arieana R.

As an artist with a social agenda of change and inclusion, it was very inspiring for me to see a group like The Education Project wanting to affect someone's life in a positive way by acting.

I feel I grew as an artist from the experience of working with Ari, who showed me a certain freshness and a different approach to the art of photography. I hope she can see this project as an opening into a future full of possibilities. No matter how many obstacles she will find, I hope she will look back with enjoyment and a passion that will give her insight and strength. I'm grateful for The Education Project; it gives me hope.

Felix Gonzalez-Torres

The purpose of life, after all, is to live it, to taste experience to the utmost,
to reach out eagerly and without fear for newer and richer experience.

— ELEANOR ROOSEVELT (1884–1962)
American stateswoman

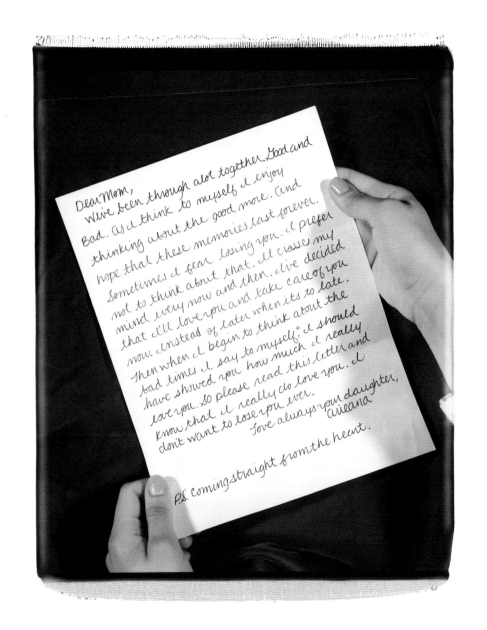

Felix Gonzalez-Torres + **Arieana R.** *Diptych*

Jean Vong + Jennifer R.

I began my relationship with Jennifer aware of not letting my ego get in the way, and wondering what kind of balance to arrive at where there could be an even amount of input from both of us. At first she was very shy and not very interested in the creative assignments I gave her between meetings. But when we actually began working with the camera, she came alive and was very excited. It was amazing to see her curiosity and to watch her experience photography. She was in awe of the camera. It became clear to me that no one had ever listened to her ideas or paid enough attention to her to take her thoughts seriously. The experience was liberating for me as well, because it freed me up to do a photograph that was beautiful without "art world committee" judgements going on in my head. It reminded me of how I took pictures when I was a teenager.

Jean Vong

I liked working with Jean, and I liked working on this project. It let me express my feelings of how water feels to me in an art form. It was more fun than I thought I would ever have. I liked thinking of the idea for the project, and I liked going shopping for props. Last, I loved setting up and taking shots of my underwater world.

Jennifer R.

It let me express my feelings of how water feels to me in an art form.

Jennifer R.

Jean Vong + Jennifer R.

Carla Weber + Zahrah L.

When I was a little girl my art had no meaning. It was just a picture to me. I thought I had no talent; I was going through a difficult and depressing time. As I started drawing, my work began to have meaning. It was totally different. I decided to go the extra mile and make others see it too. Then I got this wonderful opportunity with Carla. It made me feel special and good that other artists thought my work was good, too.

When I like my work, I feel happy and loved by Allah. My work means the world to me. Art is everything to me. My work, good or bad, takes me to another private, new and exciting world by myself. When I draw I control my dreams and create a whole new dimension. I control how it looks – how big or small – how I want it to look, what colors to use. I have power in my small world of art. I want others to explore my world and feel something for my art, something that gives them a whole new meaning. I want to share with others like me a whole new outlook, something we can talk about and share feelings about.

Zahrah L.

Zahrah's enthusiasm, talent, focus, imagination and need to express herself were all additions to what could have been a very difficult situation. Her eagerness to participate as an artist was boundless. For her there were no limits. I was there as her partner to share ideas with her, and in those first few hours we managed to cross the boundaries of fear, frustration and "adulthood."

The body of work that emanated from those intense hours spent in the Polaroid studio together was not recognizable at first. What had begun as a self-portrait for Zahrah manifested into "selves"-portraits. My image kept appearing. Always a mistake, always more provocative. I had to go back to the studio the next day to study what had happened. It was truly a surprising blend of both of our desires to emerge out of entrapment, as if we both had been bound by the weight and pressure of normalcy. Or was I just identifying with Zahrah? Reflections, texture and color created a door for us to emerge through.

Carla Weber

My work, good or bad, takes me
to another private, new and exciting
world by myself.

Zahrah L.

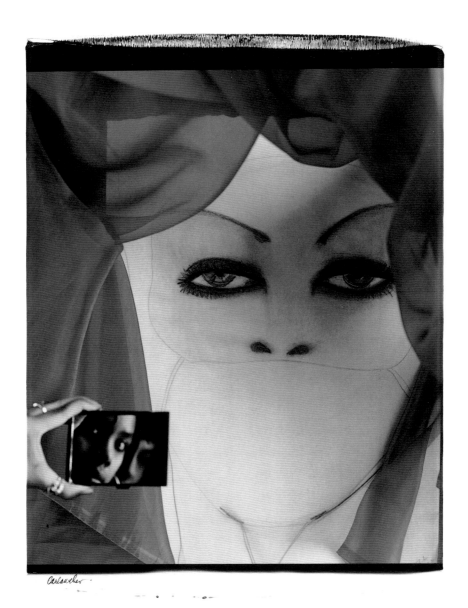

Carla Weber + **Zahrah L.**

William Wegman + Fernando Ruiz

My experience on the Polaroid 20 x 24 camera was for me the greatest thing in the world. Just thinking about working with an artist so famous and a camera so famous I felt nervous. When I was working on the backdrops for the project, I felt negative about my work. I didn't think it was my best. I didn't say anything because not all pieces an artist creates are his best, and he still has to cope with it. So that's exactly what I did. I actually think that everybody who wants to be an artist goes through this experience and ends up learning from it. I've definitely learned from this experience.

Fernando Ruiz

At first I was ambivalent about the project and was afraid I had nothing
to say to a young person from a background so different than mine. But
not wanting to appear grumpy, I abandoned caution and commenced a
series of illuminating phone conversations with Fernando. I learned of a
community of artists who are interested in teaching. Fernando is fifteen
and is keenly interested in educating young people! His enthusiasm was
infectious, and soon I was delirious with anticipation and fear. It all
worked out great. It was fun to help.

William Wegman

When I was working on the backdrops
for the project, I felt negative
about my work. I didn't think it was
my best. I didn't say anything
because not all pieces an artist creates
are his best, and he still has to cope
with it.

Fernando Ruiz

William Wegman + Fernando Ruiz

Afterword

Art Works began during a staff meeting when Janeil Engelstad, director of Public Programs and Development, suggested we approach the Polaroid Corporation about working with the Polaroid 20 x 24 inch camera. At the time, The Education Project was forging a relationship between at-risk teens and filmmakers and video artists. Working with photographers seemed like a next logical step. We met with John Reuter, director of Polaroid's 20 x 24 Studio, and Stacy Fischer the studio manager, who also coordinates special projects, and were given Polaroid's go-ahead.

The ten teenagers who participated in Art Works were chosen because they live in environments that present overwhelming obstacles and challenges. They are representatives of a much larger community of youth who are at-risk of having little or no contact with the arts, because they live in shelters for the homeless, are overcoming drug addiction, have been affected by AIDS and/or live in neighborhoods that have been devastated by unemployment and lack of public programs.

Initially, most of the teens had difficulty focusing their creative energy, something we consistently encounter in our video workshops. Often it was very difficult for them to articulate their ideas to the artists with whom they were collaborating. Our staff worked closely with them to overcome their anxieties and to clarify their ideas before their first meeting with their artist/collaborator. The teens were briefed about the artists and their work and were encouraged to take an active role in the partnership. The artists were briefed about the teens' personal histories and their particular interests in the arts. If the teens had any inhibitions, they evaporated as quickly as images appeared on film. The immediacy of the Polaroid process, like video, is a potent way of stimulating enthusiasm and a free flow of self expression. For until an idea is made real, i.e. transformed into an image or a series of images on a screen, it simply does not hold any meaning for the youth. Once a familiar and valued medium is the frame of reference, the teens become startlingly unselfconscious, spontaneous and resourceful.

While all of the teens are at-risk, their stories are very different, and each collaboration had its own unique chemistry.* Richard and Lee were two of the most outstanding teens in our video workshops. It was towards the end of baseball season when we invited Richard to participate in Art Works. What we didn't realize was how committed he was to baseball. At our first meeting, we had to spend over an hour looking for him before we found him among a hundred or more kids warming up for his team's playoffs. But things sailed along once we got past that first hurdle and were able to support Richard's desire to create work that relates to his passion for sports.

* *In a few cases, the personal histories have had to be kept confidential at the request of the youths' parents or the organization that arranged their introduction to The Education Project.*

Lee is someone with an abundance of natural ability. He is a musician, songwriter, actor, basketball player and savvy street charmer. From the first time he picked up a camera, it was obvious Lee has an eye and lots of imagination. It also became clear that things come almost too easily for him, and that he sometimes has difficulty following through.

When Lee's idea, a portrait of himself and his friends as the Four Horsemen of the Apocalypse, fell through because his friends didn't show up for the photography session, Lee rose to the occasion with another idea his face in one photo and a lion in another. Chuck Close, his collaborator, suggested a double exposure, a technique Lee wasn't aware of. Even cool Lee lost his composure when he saw his image merge with the symbol of pride and power. Lee and Chuck's photograph, with its positive message, has come to represent the project for all of us.

We became acquainted with Ishah through Lee. Ishah was the only member of the Four Horsemen to show up. As we talked with Ishah, we realized he was perfect for Art Works. A resident of the Lower East Side, Ishah has been drawing, composing and playing music since he was a young child. He has recently founded a hip-hop group and is working on a recording of his music. These accomplishments figured into his work with John Divola which combines photography with lyrics from Ishah's songs about the turmoil of life in the inner city.

Helena was introduced to us by people at the Odyssey House, a live-in drug rehabilitation center in Greenwich Village. When we first met her, we were amazed at her take-charge attitude and openness. She freely told us about her past, her failures and accomplishments and how she had been attending art workshops on Saturdays at Odyssey House. As an Art Works collaborator, she wanted to learn about portraiture and to photograph her brother, Javier, her "silent support." Helena maintains an interest in becoming an attorney so she can help others.

The Education Project

Paul's mother accompanied him to his first meeting with Andres Serrano. Paul was very shy and had a difficult time talking about his art. His mother tried to get him to open up by speaking about his gift for drawing. Much to his surprise, she told Andres how her son had been accepted into LaGuardia High School, a New York City school known for its art curriculum. This was the first time Paul had heard about his acceptance by LaGuardia; his mother had opted for enrolling him at a parochial school instead. During the meeting Paul became moody and withdrew from the conversation. Andres immediately became moderator and a mentor to Paul. A friendship was born.

Paul's mother supported him throughout the project buying him art supplies, arranging for transportation, accompanying him to the gallery where Andres was having an exhibition and to the shoot. She was so impressed by the project and Paul's accomplishments, she decided to let him attend LaGuardia, despite her commitment to a more structured education.

Other teens moved into arts education programs because of Art Works. Arieana, an aspiring graphic artist who worked with Felix Gonzalez-Torres, came up with a range of ideas for working on the camera. The night before her shoot, her mother, who was to be the subject of her photograph canceled because Arieana's younger brother became ill. Arieana was devastated. Late into the night, Janeil and Felix helped her with a new plan. After many telephone conversations, she regained her confidence by writing a letter to herself. The next day the letter became the subject of her work, underscoring how language is a form of communication and art for Arieana. Full of energy and enthusiasm Arieana is keen to learn more about photography. She will attend classes offered by the International Center of Photography, supported by Felix and The Education Project.

Sheila Divola Bergman, The Education Project's director, met Kenlly and Fernando while teaching at Sacred Heart's Middle School in the South Bronx. Kenlly, not unlike many teens her age, is interested in fashion design and popular culture. She's reliable, enthusiastic and appears not to be affected by her volatile neighborhood. Her family's apartment is filled with her father's paintings of landscapes and portraits of relatives and friends. Her interest in feminine preoccupations was a perfect match for Laurie Simmons. Through fashion illustration and drawing, Kenlly continues to explore popular culture.

Fernando is active in his community helping to organize local youths who are interested in mural painting. As part of Bronx National Artists, he regularly corresponds with other young muralists in Los Angeles, Paris and Puerto Rico. His participation in Art Works led to an invitation to work with Tim Rollins and K.O.S – Kids Of Survival – a South Bronx-based arts group which provides space for making and exhibiting art and directs and supports at-risk teens pursuing college educations.

Because of their accomplishments in art, Jennifer and Zahrah were recommended by the Montague School in Brooklyn, a program sponsored by the Jewish Board of Family and Children's Services and The New York City Board of Education. It is a day treatment center for troubled girls.

Jennifer, whose sculptures are on exhibit throughout her school, was interested in exploring natural themes, including dolphins, water and butterflies. The beauty of nature is not an escape for Jennifer, but a tool for self-exploration. With Jean Vong she created an organic dream world where water, objects and color move the viewer into her imagined space.

Zahrah, a truly gifted artist, has been drawing since she was a young girl. Her subjects range from human forms to abstract lines and shapes to fantastical clothing designs. For Zahrah, art work is critical to keeping her life together. Her collaboration with Carla began by phone, with Carla in Los Angeles and Zahrah in New York. After many conversations, they met and began what both have called a "life-changing experience." The fifteen photographs created by Zahrah and Carla show the evolution of their unique collaboration, almost as if you are looking through a window into their souls.

It is difficult to speculate about whether any of the young people who pass through Art Works will become photographers, filmmakers or video artists. Our hope is more modest: to foster an awareness that creative endeavors are an exciting and gratifying means for expression. We aim to change kids' perceptions of art as something made by and for others. To be truly committed to fostering a new generation of educators, artists and social activists that is more inclusive, The Education Project believes it is crucial to extend an invitation to all young people to witness and to participate in the creative process in a non-threatening, non-manipulative environment. Only then can they begin to understand the creative process and possibly make it a valuable part of their personal and public lives.

Sheila Divola Bergman
Janeil Engelstad
Carolyn Grifel

The Education Project

The Education Project was founded in 1991 by Sheila Divola Bergman, with the support of a handful of artists and educators who wanted to help redress the alarming state of arts education in the United States. TEP organizes workshops and informal teaching groups enabling kids and teenagers to use the film, video and photography mediums as a means of self-expression. With assistance from a dedicated group of volunteers, TEP also teaches creative writing, drawing and painting. The project focuses on individuals who, because of physical or financial difficulties, do not have access to seeing or making art. TEP also works closely with well known artists and filmmakers who give their time to work one-on-one with disadvantaged youths.

Because TEP reaches out to young people from low-income communities, efforts are made to focus students on concrete career goals and to facilitate those goals by offering internships with art professionals. Some of the teens who participated in the Art Works collaboration also worked on the production of the catalog and the installation of the exhibition. Art Works II: Taking the Next Step, the film equivalent of the Polaroid one-on-one project, is planned for 1994.

The Polaroid 20 x 24 camera – *one of five in the world – is a highly sophisticated photographic instrument that produces a full-color, 20 x 24 inch contact photograph in seventy seconds. The Polaroid camera was invented in 1948 by Edwin Land, founder of the Polaroid Corporation. Originally developed as an art historical research tool, the camera has been made available to Polaroids's Artist's Support Program.*
To this day it is used extensively by both artists and commercial clients. The 20 x 24 inch camera is six-foot-tall and weighs 235 pounds – just slightly smaller than a sub compact car. The camera's home is the Polaroid 20 x 24 Studio, located in the Soho section of New York City. Polaroid's corporate headquarters are in Cambridge, Massachusetts.

Acknowledgments

Thanks to the artists, teens and their parents. Our deepest gratitude to our board Chairperson Carolyn Grifel for her continual support of the Education Project. Thanks to Barbara Hitchcock, John Reuter and Stacy Fischer at the Polaroid Corporation whose enthusiasm and support made this project possible. Thanks to the Lannan Foundation for having faith in Art Works. We'd also like to thank Shelley Wood for photographing the collaborations and supporting our efforts. The success of this project would not have been possible without her. Carole Kismaric shared her knowledge for our first time out.

The following people and/or organizations helped us contact and keep in touch with the teens: Marion Edmonds at The Manhattan Center for the Living and Toniann Read; Donald Bennett at The Urban Family Center; Holly Markham at Lifeforce; The Jewish Board of Family and Children's Services/Montague School; Br. Armand Lamagna and Br. Steve Milan at Sacred Heart Middle School, South Bronx and Odyssey House. Thanks to Jayne H. Baum of the Jayne H. Baum Gallery, New York. Thanks to Dave Herndon and Jim Vestal at New York *Newsday*, Typogram for computer services and Aurora Color Lab.

Special thanks to Tim Rollins who wrote the essay for the Art Works catalogue and paved the way for organizations like The Education Project with his work with K.O.S. (Kids of Survival). Michael Josefowicz of Red Ink Productions and Mark Randall, catalog designer, supported the creation of this publication from the beginning. New York Foundation for the Arts, receives our deepest gratitude. Finally, we thank Sharon Cohen and James Bergman for advice and support and for putting up with our needs and hectic schedules.